SOLVING THE
PROCRASTINATION
PUZZLE

JEREMY P. TARCHER/PENGUIN
a member of Penguin Group (USA)
New York

SOLVING THE PROCRASTINATION PUZZLE

A Concise Guide to
Strategies for Change

TIMOTHY A. PYCHYL, PH.D.

JEREMY P. TARCHER/PENGUIN
Published by the Penguin Group
Penguin Group (USA) LLC
375 Hudson Street
New York, New York 10014

USA · Canada · UK · Ireland · Australia
New Zealand · India · South Africa · China

penguin.com
A Penguin Random House Company

Previously published as *The Procrastinator's Digest* in Canada
by Howling Pines Publishers in 2010
Previously published and distributed in the United States by Xlibris Publishing in 2010
First Tarcher/Penguin paperback edition 2013
Text copyright © 2010 by Timothy A. Pychyl
Comics copyright © 2010 by Timothy A. Pychyl and Paul Mason

Most Tarcher/Penguin books are available at special quantity discounts for bulk
purchase for sales promotions, premiums, fund-raising, and educational needs.
Special books or book excerpts also can be created to fit specific needs.
For details, write: Special.Markets@us.penguingroup.com.

Library of Congress Cataloging-in-Publication Data

Pychyl, Timothy A.
Solving the procrastination puzzle: a concise guide to strategies for change /
Timothy A. Pychyl, Ph.D. — First Tarcher/Penguin paperback edition.
p.   cm.
Previously published as *The Procrastinator's Digest* in Canada
by Howling Pines Publishers in 2010.
ISBN 978-0-399-16812-3
1. Procrastination.   2. Change (Psychology).   I. Title.
BF637.P76P93   2013   2013036564
179'.8—dc23

Printed in the United States of America
3   5   7   9   10   8   6   4   2

BOOK DESIGN BY EMILY S. HERRICK

SABBATICAL IS A WONDERFUL PART OF THE ACADEMIC LIFE. It is a tradition where on every seventh year scholars are given time, uninterrupted by teaching and administrative duties, to read, research, and write. I give thanks for this gift of scholarship, and I dedicate my writing to those at my university and faculty association who preserve this important tradition.

CONTENTS

ACKNOWLEDGMENTS

This book began to take shape from a collection of blog postings for *Psychology Today*. In fact, it was in writing my "Don't Delay" blog that I discovered how much I enjoyed writing to communicate ideas outside of formal scholarly journal articles. I discovered that instead of "writing to earn" in my "publish or perish" academy, I was "writing to learn" and learning to write in a whole new way. Given this beginning to the book, I want to preface my acknowledgments by giving special thanks to Lybi Ma (deputy editor of *Psychology Today* and author), who invited me to be part of the *Psychology Today* bloggers in 2008 and who has nurtured my sense of self as a writer. As well, I want to thank Hara Estroff Marano (editor at large, *Psychology Today*, and author), who, like Lybi, has always been encouraging and supportive. They are part of a truly wonderful team of people.

Writing is not a solitary activity, even though we may struggle with concepts and the words to express these ideas in our own "dark night of the soul" at times. Writing is a very social act, from the inception of ideas through to revising a final manuscript. So I have quite a few people I want to thank for helping me with my writing. Of course, as my father always told me, you can delegate the activity but not the responsibility; you can share the praise but not the blame. This means that any of the shortcomings in my writing are my own. The things that you like best about this book are most probably due to the kind input of these others who deserve my words of appreciation.

As a scholar, I have drawn on a wide body of research in my writing. Yet, unlike my scholarly publications, I have not cited this work in an academic fashion, so I want to give credit to some key individuals who have developed ideas that I have distilled in this book. In terms of the procrastination research literature specifically, my colleagues Drs. Joseph Ferrari (DePaul University, Chicago), Clarry Lay (retired, York University, Toronto), Henri Schouwenburg (retired, University of Groningen, The Netherlands), and Fuschia Sirois (Bishops University, Sherbrooke, Quebec) have provided the foundation of ideas about how best to understand procrastination. If I was not drawing on their work directly in my writing, I was speaking to some of my own research that was built on their work. I am grateful to have all of them as colleagues and friends.

In addition to the procrastination research, I drew on numerous other studies that have helped me to understand the nature of self-regulation failure, how we can structure our intentions to more successfully meet our goals, as well as aspects of our personality such as perfectionism that can undermine our goal pursuit. Although it is not possible to list everyone, I do want to note the enormous contributions made by, respectively, Drs. Roy Baumeister and Diane Tice (and their students at Florida State University), Brian Little (retired, Carleton University, Ottawa), Peter Gollwitzer (and his students at New York University), and Gordon Flett (York University, Toronto). I have learned a great deal from each of these scholars, and their work provided a framework for both understanding self-regulatory failure and strategies to more effectively exercise self-control to break nonconscious habits and patterns of behavior.

It is easy to see how these esteemed and accomplished scholars have contributed to my own thinking and research. Not so obvious, but just as important, has been the contribution of my students to my research and writing. My research is driven by my students, as research at the graduate level in particular is a means to teaching and learning. I want to thank all of my students who have participated in procrastination research with me since 1995 as part of the *Procrastination Research Group*, and I particularly want to identify the important contributions made by Shannon Bennett, Kelly Binder, Allan Blunt, Matthew Dann, Mohsen Haghbin, Eric Heward, Jennifer Lavoie, Adam McCaffrey, Rick Morin, Brian Salmon, Matthew Shanahan, Kyle Simpson, and Rachelle Thibodeau. Each of these students has taken his or her own research past the thesis requirements and into the scholarly literature more formally.

Moving from research results to communicable ideas for others to read is a craft unto itself. I am grateful for the help of my wife, Beth, who, as a nonpsychologist, is willing to ask me to clarify my ideas or my words. It takes courage for her to persist at times, I fear, because it is easy for me to become defensive about my writing. I know her thoughtful comments always make my thinking and writing clearer. In addition, my friend Jeannie Bacon, who was willing to test the strength of friendship by providing her expertise to the editing of my book, has made an important difference in my writing. Jeannie, a writer with both graduate work in English and professional experience in technical writing, helped me to be more coherent and consistent with my prose. Where you still might find problems with my writing are places where I failed to heed her helpful advice.

The comics in the book, which provide a different perspective on the concepts discussed as well as a little laughter at our all-too-human tendency to "put it off until tomorrow," are due to the talents of my friend Paul Mason. I met Paul when he was a boy and I was living one of my other lives as a canoe outfitter for *Trailhead* in Ottawa. Along with his father, Bill, and his sister, Becky, Paul has developed an international reputation for canoeing and art. I was delighted when he agreed to collaborate with me on a comic series. When a particular comic makes you laugh, you can be sure it was Paul's creative insight that captured the concept so well.

Each of the people I have identified, plus many others whom I hope I have not offended by omitting them in my words of thanks, have made readily apparent contributions to my research and writing. My final words of thanks are to those whose contributions are more obscure in terms of the writing of this book, yet deeply important to me personally. They make life joyful, provide room for my writing, and bring balance to my life.

My children, Laurel and Alex, along with my wonderful wife, Beth, bring love and laughter to my life. I work hard not to procrastinate on the more mundane tasks in my day simply to be sure that there is time for them! My dog team keeps me firmly grounded and in the great outdoors enough to keep me healthy and happy. Finally, my father, Walter Pychyl, is never far from my thoughts and I draw on his wisdom, love, and support to build a life. Ironically, one of my dad's most often-used expressions is "We'll see what happens" as he waits another day to act. I usually laugh and say to him, "No wonder I study procrastination!" Yet within his words is a great deal of wisdom. Sometimes delay may truly be wise and the best course of action. Knowing the difference between procrastination and other forms of delay is a very good place to start. You'll find some of the reasons why beginning in Chapter 1.

INTRODUCTION

If you are reading this, it is probably because you are bothered by procrastination.

You may be even be reading this because you are procrastinating right now. You are avoiding some other task. I want to make the time you spend off task, right now, worthwhile.

That is the purpose of my writing. An hour from now, you will be prepared to act differently. You will be prepared to be more successful in your goal pursuit.

Are you ready to get started? That is one of my most basic strategies: just get started. In this book, I explain why this works and summarize the research evidence for such a simple, practical strategy.

About This Book

This is a short book—practical and no-nonsense. Although as short as possible, each concept, topic, and issue presented has been carefully researched.

I have been researching and writing about procrastination for nearly twenty years. You can learn about my research at procrastination.ca. This Web site provides access to my research group and academic publications, as well as my iProcrastinate Podcasts and "Don't Delay" blog for *Psychology Today*. I have had millions of downloads of my podcasts and blog entries. Like this book, these resources are research-based but meant to be very accessible for people who do not normally read psychological research.

The key difference between my blog or podcast and this book is the organization of the ideas. The blog and podcast cover a wide variety of important topics, but you would have to spend days reading or listening to get it all. *The value of this book is that it is a digest of my research, and most important, this book provides a concise summary of key strategies to reduce procrastination in your life.*

Why Is the Book So Short?

Too often, we start a book, read the first chapter or two, and never pick it up again (although we intend to finish it!). Among procrastinators, this is a terrible risk. In fact, procrastination is defined by this intention-action gap. I do not want to contribute to this, so I have written a short book. It is possible to read the whole thing in a few hours (fast readers may get through the main ideas and key strategies in an hour, in fact).

Most important, I have written a short book because I believe that less is more. It is quite possible for me to write hundreds of pages about this topic. I have in my blog and research, for example. My graduate students regularly write lengthy theses on the topic. However, when it comes to learning strategies for change, a few key ideas are what is required. Working with these ideas in your own life will make a difference. Your reading can make a difference in your life right now—if you want it to.

"If you want it to." This idea is very important to understand. No technique on its own will ever work without a firm commitment to a goal. *If you are committed to change, I know that what you will learn here will make a difference.* I have received emails from people from all walks of life (e.g., lawyers, students, homemakers, consultants, medical researchers, and even other academics) and from all over the world that attest to the difference that these strategies are making in their lives.

How the Book Is Organized

I have structured each chapter in a similar way so that the book is easier and quicker to read. You know what to expect in each chapter.

First, I begin each chapter with a key phrase that may become your mantra for change. A mantra is an often-repeated expression or idea. It is commonly associated with meditation as the focus of your thoughts. I think the first sentence of every chapter can serve you best as a daily focus as you work toward change in your life.

When you read a chapter that really speaks to you in terms of your own procrastination, memorize the opening mantra for change; post it on your fridge or on your computer as a screen saver. In short, make it your own and reflect on it often.

Second, I offer an example through a short story that highlights a common problem with procrastination. These stories are based on lived experiences shared with me by research participants, as replies to my blog postings and podcasts, as well as through people I have met at invited talks, workshops, and even at social gatherings (these are people who tell me that they would be the perfect subject for my studies). I hope these stories help situate the issue in lived experience for you.

Third, I summarize the key issue(s) illustrated in the story. Here, I draw on research, but I do not quote dates, names, or other details as I do in my academic papers, blog, or podcasts. I write about the issue and research in simple terms to keep the concepts clear. When I do introduce a term from research, some psychological jargon, I explain what it means.

Fourth, based on the research, I present strategies that you might use to facilitate change in your life. These strategies flesh out the mantra at the beginning of the chapter, linking the issue and what we know from research to things you can do to reduce your procrastination. These strategies are the practical things that you can do to solve the procrastination puzzle in your own life.

As appropriate, I also provide a place for you to rephrase the key ideas in relation to your own life. This is where you make the concepts your own in the context of your own life. This is where you do your first bit of personal work and goal setting.

Finally, you will find at least one comic in each chapter. Paul Mason (an artist, creative genius, and all-around great guy) and I created this series of comics together.

In the comics, we embrace the notion of carpe diem. The Latin expression *carpe diem* (which means, literally, "seize the day") has been used for centuries with contrasting meanings. For example, it has been used to celebrate and defend procrastination with a focus on enjoying the moment—"Eat, drink, and be merry, for tomorrow you may die"—and it has also been used as an admonition, scolding ourselves to focus on the pressing task at hand with expressions such as "make hay while the sun shines."

Our comics allow us to laugh at our propensity to put it off, while lamenting the tragedy of our inability to seize the day and accomplish our goals. Laugh or cry, we hope you will enjoy the situations we portray. Although the context for these comics is college and university life, I think you will find the themes applicable to other life domains.

OK, enough by way of introduction. Let's just get started.

What is procrastination?

What Is Procrastination?
Why Does It Matter?

All procrastination is delay, but not all delay is procrastination.

MARIA, A WORKING MOTHER of three young children, reaches the end of her day with lots left to do. Again, she didn't get the laundry put away or the files sorted in her office. She beats herself up, calling herself a procrastinator, yet she's confused about how she'll ever be able to get it all done when so much happens each day that's out of her control. She plans carefully, but kids' illness, changes at the day care, and both her and her husband's travel for work always seem to necessitate change in her plans and delays on some tasks.

Issue

These examples in Maria's life should *not* be seen as procrastination. We all have to delay things. Delay is part of making priorities. Of course, a child's illness takes precedence over much of what we might plan that day. Other tasks need to be delayed to make time for doctor's appointments, home care, whatever is necessary. The key issue here is that it is not a voluntary delay in the strictest sense.

Procrastination is *the voluntary delay of an intended action despite the knowledge that this delay may harm the individual in terms of the task performance or even just how the individual feels about the task or him- or herself.* Procrastination is a *needless voluntary delay.* In Maria's case, the delay on putting away the laundry and filing were not truly voluntary. She was not needlessly taking on some alternative task to avoid the laundry or filing. She was optimizing her use of time to meet one of *her* most important life goals: to be the best mother she can.

There are many types of delay in our lives. I believe we need to learn to appreciate this. Some delays are not only necessary, as with the example of Maria's task delay in favor of her children's health, they are wise. We might also decide to delay action on a project because we need more information first. It is wise to put things off at times rather than act impulsively or hastily.

Delay is a necessary part of our lives. At any given moment, there are any number of things we could do. What will we choose to do? This choice is based partly on our earlier intentions, our plans for the day, but of course, our choice will also depend on the context of the moment. What is happening right now that has an effect on our choices? What is most important now? What is the wisest thing we can do given our goals, responsibilities, roles, and desires?

Procrastination, in contrast to other forms of delay, is that voluntary and quite deliberate turning away from an intended action even when we know we could act on our intention right now. There is nothing preventing us from acting in a timely manner *except our own reluctance to act*.

This is the puzzling aspect of procrastination. Why are we reluctant to act? Why is it we become our own worst enemy?

We undermine our own goal pursuit needlessly. *Why?* How can we solve this procrastination puzzle?

To understand the procrastination puzzle—that voluntary but needless delay in our lives that undermines our goal pursuit— *we need to understand this reluctance to act when it is in our best interest to act*. We also need to have strategies to overcome this reluctance.

The conscious use of strategies to overcome our reluctance to act is essential, because procrastination for many people is a habit.

That is, procrastination is a habitual response to tasks or situations, and like all habits it is an internalized, nonconscious process. It is what we do without really thinking about it. In fact, cross-cultural research by Joseph Ferrari at DePaul University (Chicago) has demonstrated that for as much as 20 percent of the population, this procrastination habit is quite chronic and affects many parts of our lives.

Habits are not easy to change. We need to make conscious effort with specific strategies for change to be successful. Throughout the book, I argue that we need to make *predecisions* to act in a different way, counter to the habitual response. Based largely on the work of Peter Gollwitzer (New York University), I emphasize many different ways that we can use predecisions to act when we intend to act, to reduce the effects of potential distractions, and to cope more effectively with setbacks and disappointments as we work toward changing our behavior.

In the chapters that follow, I explain why we may be reluctant to act on our intentions. Then I offer strategies for change to help develop more effective self-regulation by breaking habitual ways of responding. The purpose of this introductory chapter is to emphasize that not all delay is procrastination, and the importance of focusing on the needless delay that is undermining us.

STRATEGIES FOR CHANGE

My initial strategy for change is for you to begin to categorize in your own mind which delays in your life are procrastination. These are the delays that you want to do something about. Knowing this difference is a good place to start.

As you begin to identify which delays are truly voluntary delays that undermine your performance and well-being, you may see a pattern emerge. These tasks, projects, or intended actions may have something in common. For example, you may find that these tasks, projects, or intended actions elicit common feelings.

In the table that follows (or on a separate piece of paper, or on your computer, or simply as a thought experiment), list those tasks, projects, activities, or "things" in your life on which you tend to procrastinate. Next to each, jot down what emotions and thoughts come to mind when you think of each of these moments

of procrastination. Do not overthink this. It could be, for example, that you are uncertain about what to do to complete a task.

When you have finished your list, look for patterns in the emotions or thoughts involved. You will want to refer back to these when reading some of the chapters that follow.

TASK, PROJECT, GOAL, ACTIVITY	FEELINGS AND THOUGHTS ABOUT THIS TASK/GOAL

2

Is Procrastination Really a Problem?
What Are the Costs of Procrastinating?

✛

Procrastination is failing to get on with life itself.

I ATTENDED A CONFERENCE a few summers ago titled Living Well and Dying Well: New Frontiers of Positive Psychology, Therapy, and Spiritual Care. During a discussion of coping with death and counseling individuals who are grieving, one of the psychologists in attendance noted two kinds of regrets that people express in their grief over the loss of a loved one: regrets of commission and omission. The second regret, the things we omitted doing while our loved one was alive, captured my interest. Regrets of omission are so often the result of procrastination.

I asked this psychologist, "What is the nature of these regrets of omission?" adding, "Are these:

1. Things people really intended to do but never did (i.e., procrastination)?
2. Generalized possibilities of what they could have done?
3. Cultural scripts of what they think they should have done, what would have been nice to do?
4. Internalized expectations about what the loved one might have wanted them to do?"

The psychologist replied that all four types were part of the regrets he had seen in his practice.

So I pushed on a little further and asked which type of regret seemed most problematic. As I expected, given the guilt associated with procrastination, regret over the things these grieving people really intended to do but did not was most problematic. *The regrets of omission related to our procrastination were most troubling in the grieving process.*

Issue

Everyone procrastinates. I believe this, and research has documented this in a number of different ways. In fact, I think that people who say that they have never procrastinated might also say that they have never told a lie or been rude to someone. It is possible, I guess, but unlikely. We certainly do not like to admit to these undesirable actions.

So, if everyone procrastinates, why is it a problem?

The research evidence is clear. People who score high on self-report measures of procrastination also self-report lower achievement overall, more negative feelings, and even significantly more health problems. Let me discuss each of these briefly.

The lower achievement is easy to explain. Although we can all remember instances where we procrastinated and did very well (we cherish these memories to make us feel better and to justify even more procrastination), on the whole, procrastination results in less time to do a thorough job. This usually means poorer work overall. A meta-analysis of the procrastination research conducted by Piers Steel (University of Calgary) has shown that procrastination is certainly never helpful and usually harmful to our task performance.

The fact that procrastination is associated with more negative emotions (or moods) is puzzling. If we are procrastinating, you would think we would actually feel better because we are not doing the tasks we do not want to do in favor of things we enjoy. At least that is what you would think we are doing.

The thing is, our research shows that even when we are procrastinating, and I mean when we are actually off task and researchers ask us questions then about our feelings, we do not report feeling happier necessarily. There is a mixture of feelings experienced, including guilt. So, on the whole, procrastination does not make us feel that great, and this is particularly true in the long run.

Finally, the new research by Fuschia Sirois (Bishops University, Sherbrooke, Quebec) that demonstrates that procrastination actually compromises our health is very interesting. Procrastination seems to affect health in two ways. First, procrastination causes stress, which is not a good thing for our health for many reasons (e.g., stress compromises our immune systems).

Second, chronic procrastinators needlessly delay health behaviors such as exercising, eating healthfully, and getting enough sleep. This affects our health negatively, particularly over time. Sure, not exercising today or not eating vegetables today is not going to harm us today. But you know how it goes: Tomorrow is the same situation, we rationalize one more day of delay, and before we know it, it has been years of neglected (procrastinated) health behaviors. The results can be devastating, with increased risk for heart disease, diabetes, and other debilitating illnesses that can be prevented with more daily attention to simple but avoided health behaviors.

The day-to-day delay on small but cumulatively important tasks affects us in other ways as well. A good example is retirement savings. It is easy to put off saving to another day, but this procrastination costs us in the long run.

All of this is true about procrastination—it is seldom helpful (but we certainly recall when it is), and it is usually harmful to our task performance, psychological well-being, and even our physical health. Although all of these outcomes are negative, this is *not* what might concern us most about the consequences of procrastination.

Procrastination is a problem with not getting on with life itself. When we procrastinate on our goals, *we are our own worst enemy.* These are *our* goals, *our* tasks, and we are *needlessly putting them off.* Our goals are the things that make up a good portion of our lives. In fact, both philosophers and psychologists have proposed that happiness is found in the pursuit of our goals. It is not necessarily that we are accomplishing anything in particular, but that we are engaged in the pursuit of what we think is meaningful in our lives.

When we procrastinate on our goals, we are basically putting off our lives. We are certainly wasting the time we could be using toward our goal pursuit. The thing is, the most finite, limited resource in our lives is time. We only have a finite amount of time to live. Why waste it? Why waste it running away from tasks that we want or need to do?

Let's return for a moment to the story I told at the beginning of this chapter. As I listened to psychologists present their research papers and therapists talk about the grieving process, I left each session more convinced of the importance of dealing with procrastination as a symptom of an existential malaise, a malaise that can only be addressed by our deep commitment to authoring the stories of our lives.

To author our own lives, we have to be an active agent in our lives, not a passive participant making excuses for what we are not doing. *When we learn to stop needless, voluntary delay in our lives, we live more fully.*

It is time to make a commitment to engaging in your life, achieving your goals, and enjoying the journey. Time is too precious to waste.

STRATEGY FOR CHANGE

One of the most important preconditions for successful change is a deep commitment to that change. You really have to value that change. So I want to focus your attention on the costs of your procrastination to enhance your goal commitment.

Take a moment now to think about the list of tasks that you came up with at the end of Chapter 1. Recall that these were the tasks (goals, projects) on which you are procrastinating. I have provided a table below into which you may want to copy this list of tasks (or goals) in the first column. You may want to add new ones, too, after reading this chapter and thinking further about procrastination. I do realize that every reader is different and that you may not want to write this out. If not, stick with this as a thought experiment and just think through the next little bit.

Next to each of these tasks or goals, note how your procrastination has affected you in terms of things such as your happiness, stress, health, finances, relationships, and so on. You may even want to discuss this with a confidante or a significant other in your life who knows you well. In fact, you may be surprised by what they may have to say about the costs of procrastination in your life. Like tobacco smoke, there are secondhand effects of procrastination of which you may be unaware, including broken promises, unfulfilled obligations, and the added burden to others of "picking up the pieces" while you are busy with your last-minute efforts . . . again.

In short, it is important to recognize and acknowledge all of the costs associated with the self-regulation failure we commonly call procrastination. This knowledge can be helpful in maintaining your commitment to change.

What I expect you will see in this list is how much you are paying for your procrastination. The reward of following through with your reading today is to learn how to eliminate these unnecessary costs in your life.

Strengthening Goal Intentions

It is one thing to know the cost of not acting; it is quite another to have a strong commitment to the goal itself. A strong goal intention, an intention for which you have a very strong commitment, is absolutely essential. As is commonly said, where there's a will, there's a way.

To strengthen a goal intention, it is important to recognize the benefits of acting now, not just the costs of needless delay. Taking time to think about how your goals align with your values and larger, longer-term life goals, or simply the short-term benefit of getting a necessary task done, can be an important step in strengthening goal intentions. The last column of the table provides space for this reflection. Add notes about why this goal or task is important to get done, as well as the benefits of acting now as opposed to later.

Finally, knowing something is different from realizing it—making it real—in our lives. For example, we can understand that health habits such as regular exercise or eating low-fat foods and less refined sugar are good for us. However, we can fail to act on this knowledge until something makes this information *real* in *our* lives. A common example of this is the strengthening of goal intentions for health behaviors following the diagnosis of a serious illness such as cardiovascular disease. With the diagnosis, the knowledge of the link between behavior and health outcomes becomes real in our lives, not just knowledge about the world in general.

The trouble is, it can be too late to act at this point, and waiting for an epiphany of this sort is not the most effective life strategy. It is very important to regularly examine our intentions as a starting point to reducing procrastination. To the extent that we can strengthen our goal intentions, we are much more likely to act in a timely manner.

TASK, PROJECT, GOAL, ACTIVITY	COSTS ASSOCIATED WITH PROCRASTINATION	BENEFITS OF ACTING IN A TIMELY FASHION

3

What's the Most Important Thing We Need to Know about Procrastination?

✛

I won't give in to feel good. Feeling good now comes at a cost.

MARTIN SAID THAT he would work on the report this morning. That was yesterday, and it felt good to put that awful task off until tomorrow. Now he is facing the task and he feels awful. He is anxious and frustrated. He really dislikes this report. Feeling a whole range of negative emotions, he decides to work on some other, less important stuff instead. His mood lifts as he pushes the report aside for another day.

Issue

As the work of Roy Baumeister and Diane Tice (Florida State University) has clearly shown, procrastination is a form of *self-regulation failure*. We fail to regulate our behavior to achieve our own goals. We make an intention to act, but we do not use the self-control necessary to act when intended. This is the voluntary nature of the delay that I stressed in the first chapter that characterizes procrastination. We may voluntarily delay our action because we are unable or *unwilling* to self-regulate our behavior to act now.

There are many types of self-regulation problems, including problem gambling, overeating, reckless spending, and drinking too much. Procrastination is best understood as a problem like these—a problem with our self-regulation.

Why do we fail to self-regulate? Although there are many factors that contribute to this, the most important thing to understand is that we "give in to feel good." That is, we want to feel good now and we will do whatever it takes for immediate mood repair, usually at the expense of long-term goals.

When we give in to feel good, we give in to impulsive urges. These urges can take many forms. We might gamble, shop, or eat more than we need, ingest mood-altering substances, or procrastinate—all in an effort to avoid negative emotions. Of course, my focus is on how we use procrastination—needless task delay—to give in to feel good.

When facing a task we intend to do but do not want to, we feel a number of possible negative emotions. We may feel frustrated, angry, bored, resentful, depressed, anxious, or guilty. These emotions may be some of the emotions that you listed in your table at the end of Chapter 1. Generally, we call this *task aversiveness*. Aversive tasks are things that we all want to put off. They make us feel bad. We do not like doing these tasks.

Who really *wants to* do an aversive task? No one. However, the task may be necessary for us to reach a desired goal. We may not want to do the task, but we need to do it.

The key issue is that for chronic procrastinators, short-term mood repair takes precedence. Chronic procrastinators want to eliminate the negative mood or emotions now, so they give in to feel good. They give in to the impulse to put off the task until another time. Now, not faced with the task, they feel better.

If you find that you are chronically procrastinating, it may well be that you are running away from negative feelings by putting off your tasks. Of course, this is temporarily rewarding. The moment we put off the task until tomorrow, we feel relief from the negative emotions. And, as you may have learned in a basic psychology course, behaviors that are rewarded get repeated. We are reinforcing our procrastination, and it becomes a problem.

STRATEGIES FOR CHANGE

The issue of short-term mood repair in favor of long-term goal pursuit is a crucial one when it comes to addressing our procrastination. It is important to recognize that giving in to feel good is at the heart of self-regulation failure, and it is important to develop strategies for change.

I want to begin with the most basic, and perhaps least palatable, strategy that I can think of in relation to giving in to feel good. That is, when faced with a task where our natural inclination is to say, "I'll do this later" or "I'll feel more like this tomorrow," we need to stop and recognize that we are saying this in order to avoid the negative emotions we are feeling right now.

Knowledge is power in this regard. First and foremost, we need to recognize that this task makes us feel awful and what we are trying to do is to run away from these feelings. Of course, this takes a certain amount of *emotional intelligence*. This type of intelligence is not related to the size of our vocabulary or the ability to do arithmetic. Emotional intelligence is the ability to effectively identify and utilize emotions to guide behavior. Recent research has shown that lower emotional intelligence is related to more procrastination, but the good news is that we can increase our emotional intelligence. We can learn to more effectively perceive, understand, and regulate our emotions. This is very important in terms of more effective self-control.

In any case, based on what I know about procrastination, it seems clear that most people who procrastinate are emotionally aware enough to recognize that some tasks make them feel awful and that they are procrastinating to escape these emotions. What may require further focus and strengthening is the ability to regulate emotions, or at least some commitment not to take the path of least resistance—that is, not to give in to feel good.

What we really need to do is to come to terms with our negative feelings about a task. We need to find a way to cope with these negative feelings so that we can continue to pursue our intended goal. The question is, how?

While I was writing this book, Ivy, a podcast listener, wrote to me to say that she had developed some of her own mantras related to the iProcrastinate Podcasts. Here's what she developed on this topic:

"Don't give in to feel good, step on up to what should."

I like this type of mantra or slogan, as you know. It can help us focus more on changing our procrastination habit. Ivy's mantra could easily replace the one I offered at the beginning of this chapter.

This tough strategy is immediately effective as a first step. We have to "suck it up," as they say. Yes, we are feeling awful about the task at hand. We would rather run away, give in to feel good. However, *the first step at the moment of procrastination is to stay put.* If you turn away in an effort to make yourself feel better, it's over.

Certainly, staying put and dealing with these initial negative emotions is not the whole solution, but it is an absolutely necessary first step.

The key to success with this emotional experience is to be prepared. I will explain just why I am urging you to prepare in a certain way later. For now, I just want you to think about the following as your first step in an antiprocrastination strategy:

THINK: IF I feel negative emotions when I face the task at hand, THEN I will stay put and not stop, put off a task, or run away.

This "if . . . then" format of an intention has been labeled an *implementation intention* by Peter Gollwitzer (New York University).

I will have more to say about implementation intentions in a later chapter. At the moment, the key thing is that you need to internalize this implementation intention in order to take a first step related to the negative emotions that are associated with procrastination.

Although I think most of us have to recognize that we might very well have to just experience the first moments of these negative emotions, we do *not* simply have to take a tough-guy approach and "suck it up" to succeed. There is another, gentler approach we can take.

Essentially, it comes down to choosing the emotions on which we will focus. For example, although the dominant emotion at the moment may be fear—we may *have* fear—the key thing is that we do not have to *be* our fear. We can acknowledge this fear but choose to continue to pursue our goals working from some other part of our self. Parker Palmer, one of my favorite educational writers, speaks of this as working from some other part of our "inner landscape." Our inner landscape, the psychology of self, is more than the fear we may be experiencing. It also includes our curiosity, our desire to succeed, and another very strong emotion, our interest.

If we choose to acknowledge our fear but find "the courage to be" *in spite of this fear*, to work from another part of our inner landscape, we may more successfully stay put and stay on task. *We will not give in to feel good*. We will have made the first step toward beating procrastination.

Of course, we are quite expert at finding reasons not to persist like this. In the face of negative emotions, we might even try to justify why we want to run away. We will not acknowledge our fear or frustration. We might simply think, "I'll feel more like doing this tomorrow." We probably won't. I think we all know this deep down. This is part of the strangely puzzling nature of procrastination. We have become our own worst enemy, and we even know how to lie to ourselves.

Emotionally, we are giving in to feel good while justifying this choice by thinking, "I'll feel more like doing this tomorrow." No, we won't! In the next chapter, I explain why.

4

Why We Won't Feel Like It Tomorrow

I won't feel more like doing it tomorrow.

TO INTRODUCE THIS CHAPTER, I want to share a story I received from a reader of my *Psychology Today* blog. It clearly illustrates the problem of tomorrow. This reader said that the issue of feeling more like it tomorrow was reminiscent of a sign in a butcher's shop window in his grandparents' village in Poland.

Translated into English, the sign read: "Today you pay and tomorrow you get it for free."

When the customers would come tomorrow for their free goods, the butcher would say, "Read the sign: Today you pay, tomorrow it's free." As this reader noted, it is pretty much that way with procrastination. The tomorrow in which "I'll really feel like it" is always a day away. It never becomes today.

Issue

The story above captures the basic issue with procrastination: I'll do it tomorrow. In fact, the Latin roots of the word *procrastination* mean "to put forward to tomorrow." Yet, as the butcher explained with his sign, that tomorrow never really comes.

As with the butcher's sign that implied that customers would get free goods tomorrow, our thinking plays a trick, too. We think, "I'll feel more like it tomorrow." What we need to understand, so as not to be tricked like the butcher's customers, is why this is not true. We will not feel more like it tomorrow.

Research, particularly studies by Dan Gilbert (Harvard University) and Tim Wilson (University of Virginia), indicates that we are not very good forecasters. No, I don't mean weather forecasters. Meteorologists seem to be better at forecasting the weather (at least in the short term) than we are at forecasting our own mood in the future. Forecasting our future mood is known as *affective forecasting*.

The main idea behind affective forecasting is that we have a bias when we predict future mood (affective) states in relation to positive or negative events. For example, a couple of years after winning a lottery, the winners were about as happy as they were before their win, despite the general affective forecast that they would be much happier if only they could win the lottery. This is also true of people who have suffered debilitating accidents. A few years after the accident, despite long-term effects such as paralysis, accident victims were about as happy as they were before this life-changing event—again, despite the general affective forecast that they would be much unhappier.

Two concepts are used to explain these peculiar findings: *focalism* and *presentism*. Focalism is the tendency to underestimate the extent to which other events will influence our thoughts and feelings in the future. Presentism, as you might guess, addresses the fact that we put too much emphasis on the present in our prediction of the future. Taken together, this means that we focus on our current situation and how we feel *now* without enough consideration about the future situation, what might happen and how we might feel then (or have in similar situations in the past).

Here are some common experiences of this: If we go grocery shopping just after a meal, we will generally underestimate how much we will eat in the week ahead and buy less. Addicts who have just ingested their drug of choice will underestimate how much they will crave the drug later. Irrationally, we think how we are feeling now is how we will feel later. The most astonishing thing about this is that it is true for simple things like current and future hunger states.

HOW IS THIS RELATED TO PROCRASTINATION?

We need to consider what this human bias in affective forecasting means to our understanding of procrastination. By this point, the argument may be apparent. In making an intention for future action, we focus on our current affective state with the mistaken assumption that our affective state at the point we expect to act on our intention will be the same as it is now.

The real catch here is that *when we intend a future action, our affective state is often particularly positive.* Why? There are two reasons.

First, because we are putting off action until the future, we get the reward that we discussed with giving in to feel good. We feel good now that the intention is for *future* action. At the very least, we feel relief that we are not on the hook to act now.

Second, we are imagining ourselves engaged in some future

action that we perceive will make us happy. This is pleasant in and of itself. Health behaviors are good examples here. If we intend to go for a run tomorrow, we feel good about ourselves for making such a proactive health-related intention. Good for us! Our current affective state is positive, and we incorrectly forecast that our affective state tomorrow at the intended time of the run will be the same.

There is nothing like a righteous intention now for action later to make us feel good. "I'll run tomorrow." "I'll do that assignment tomorrow." "I'll write that report later." Happiness now, pay later (or not, as the case may be). Unless we can get better at "mental time traveling," where we can set intentions with clearer knowledge about how we will feel about taking action in the future, we will continue to be predictably irrational with our procrastination.

STRATEGIES FOR CHANGE

We need a two-pronged approach to increase the likelihood that we will act on our intentions. One strategy is "time travel." The other is to expect to be wrong and deal with it.

STRATEGY #1—*Time Travel*

As numerous psychologists who study affective forecasting have advocated, we need to use mental images of the future more often and more accurately. We need to represent the future as though it were happening in the present. For example, a person who is procrastinating on saving for retirement might imagine as vividly as possible living on his or her potential retirement savings. To make a future image like this more concrete and accurate, it may be important to set out some numbers for a budget and take into account the reality of the need for, and increasing expense of, health care in old age. This "time travel" can help make our predictions of the future more accurate and motivate us to take more appropriate action now.

Unfortunately, I am not that confident that this approach will work for many people. First, it is possible that we will put off this planning task itself, a form of *second-order procrastination*. Second, even if we do this task, the initial emotional response (e.g., fear) will most likely wear off quickly, and, more important, the fact that retirement is so far away may still result in our discounting its importance and delaying our savings further.

STRATEGY #2—*Expect to Be Wrong and Deal with It*

This second strategy is more effective, but you may think that is a hard-nosed approach. In this case, rather than trying to change what seems to be a deeply ingrained bias in human thinking by improving our affective forecasts, *I think we should simply learn to expect to be wrong and go from there.* We do this every day with respect to weather forecasts, and most recently we have been learning to do this with ridiculously inaccurate economic forecasts.

Given our ability to cope with inaccurate meteorological and economic forecasts, I have confidence we can cope effectively with our poor affective forecasting. This strategy, by necessity, takes two forms or approaches.

APPROACH #1

When we are tempted to procrastinate on a current intention or task, thinking that we'll feel more like it tomorrow, we need to stop and think, "No, that's a problem with my forecasting. There is a good chance I won't feel more like it tomorrow." AND it is important to add the following:

"My current motivational state does not need to match my intention in order to act."

This is a common misconception about goal pursuit: We believe that we have to actually feel like it. We don't. And, with many of the tasks in our lives, we won't feel like it . . . ever! The thing is, our motivational state does not need to match the intention. We can do something even if we do not feel like it. Parents spend a lot of time explaining this to their children.

Here is another example: Much as we might prefer a sunny day to go out for a run or a bike ride, we can put on rain gear and get outside. In fact, successful athletes do this every day. They are not "fair-weather trainers." The weather does not have to match the activity. We can cope with what we get and still act as intended.

Similarly, acknowledging that our motivational state is neither necessary nor sufficient to ensure action, we can simply remind ourselves of our personal goals (a form of self-affirmation) and "just get started." Progress will fuel well-being and enhance goal attainment (more on this in Chapter 6).

APPROACH #2

When we set an intention to act tomorrow, and tomorrow comes, *expect that you probably will not feel overly enthused to get started.* Given that our intention was made yesterday (or much earlier) with the optimistic mood that comes with having a plan, we will probably feel less happy than we expected with the reality of the task now at hand (again, this is all part of our biased affective forecasting).

Now, *the thing to do is to remember that this is a transient mood* and think through all of the issues raised with Approach #1, particularly how your motivational state does not need to match the task for you to get started right now.

This is "tough love" with oneself, I suppose. Certainly, many of us have heard this advice as we were growing up. It was couched in terms of "maturity" and the "responsibilities of adulthood." These were often expressions of tough love, too. This was advice from adults in our lives who were trying to nurture fortitude and realism with respect to willpower.

In sum, the strategy I am advocating for dealing with our bias toward thinking we'll feel more like it tomorrow is knowing that this is a common problem with being human. We are not very good at predicting how we will feel in the future. We are overly optimistic, and our optimism comes crashing down when tomorrow comes. When our mood sours, we end up where I started in the last chapter, giving in to feel good. We procrastinate.

The problem is pretty obvious, as is the solution: *Let go of the misconception that our motivational state must match the task at hand.* In fact, social psychologists have demonstrated that attitudes follow behaviors more than (or at least as much as) behaviors follow attitudes. When you start to act on your intention as intended, you will see your attitude and motivation change.

This gets me a little bit ahead of our story, however. For now, let's keep the focus on the mantra for this chapter: "I won't feel more like doing it tomorrow."

5

Excuses and Self-Deception:
How Our Thinking Contributes
to Our Procrastination

I need to be aware of my rationalizations.

ALLAN LAMENTED HIS PROCRASTINATION to anyone who would listen, but nothing seemed to change. His friends recognized him as the master of excuses, although Allan didn't acknowledge his own hidden talents here. He was truly the "Teflon guy" when it came to being accountable, even to himself. Nothing stuck to him. There was always an excuse for waiting another day, and there was always an excuse for being off task.

It's not due for weeks.

I can do that work in a few hours.

I work better under pressure.

Of course, another day always became another, and soon weeks or months passed without progress. Why couldn't Allan see how he was just rationalizing this needless delay?

Issue

In addition to understanding our basic impulse to give in to feel good (see Chapter 3) and not really feel more like doing it tomorrow (see Chapter 4), we need to consider some of the biases in our thinking. There are a number of very important issues to consider, including the human tendency to:

1. discount future rewards in relation to short-term rewards,

2. underestimate the time things will take and overestimate how much we can do,

3. prefer tomorrow over today,

4. self-handicap to protect self-esteem,

5. think irrationally about the task at hand and our ability to accomplish the task, and

6. manufacture our own happiness by changing our thinking to be consistent with our behavior.

Books have been written about each of these topics, but true to the digest nature of this book (and the promise to provide you with what you need now), I have summarized each of these problems in the sections below. Of course, this is followed by strategies for change.

Discounting Future Rewards over Short-Term Rewards

Future rewards, particularly those in the more distant future, seem smaller in size. It is as if we are looking at a picture of a distant mountain and assuming that it is actually small. We do not seem to have perspective for size when time is involved. This is the notion of discounting future rewards, also known as *temporal discounting*.

The problem is that future rewards seem less attractive to us than immediately available ones. I guess this should not surprise us too much. From an evolutionary perspective, a bird in the hand is worth two in the bush. Our brains seem programmed to prefer immediate rewards. This stone-age brain is not so adaptive in our modern world, where we need to meet distant deadlines by doing things today.

The Planning Fallacy

It is also human nature to be overly optimistic. We assume we can get more done in less time than is reasonable, and we assume tasks will take less time than they usually do. This is at the heart of the issue—we are not really thinking about how long things usually take based on past experience. We focus on the *singular* event we are facing without taking into account *distributive* information about experience or similar events. What results from this optimistic bias is poor planning.

Self-Handicapping to Protect Self

To self-handicap is to provide an excuse for oneself. For example, if you were to wear weighted shoes and have a running race with a friend, your ability or competence as a runner would never come into question. If you lose the race, it is the fault of the handicap, the heavy shoes. If you win the race, however, that is extraordinarily meritorious. It is win-win for the individual's sense of self. Certainly, self-esteem is never threatened.

A similar situation can arise with procrastination. To the extent that we delay work on a task to the last moment, we can be creating another form of self-handicapping. As with the running race, a task done at the last minute can be excused if not done well because it was done in such a short amount of time. And, of course, if the task is done very well, it looks exceptionally good for the individual.

This implies that the needless delay of a task that we defined as procrastination may in fact fill a need. It can protect self-esteem, and experimental research evidence by Joseph Ferrari (DePaul University) indicates that chronic procrastinators in particular prefer not to have feedback about self if they have the choice. Of course, delay of this sort has begged the question of whether this is truly procrastination at all, because it can be seen as a strategic use of delay, but it is worth including here just to acknowledge that we can end up delaying our tasks for reasons that may not at first seem apparent.

SOLVING THE PROCRASTINATION PUZZLE

Preferring Tomorrow over Today

Here is an example of a relation that we all understand: If B is greater than A, and C is greater than B, then we can assume that C is also greater than A. This is known as a *transitive relation*.

What about this example? Imagine a task is due on Friday. It is now Monday morning. It is preferable to work on this task Tuesday as opposed to Monday. In other words, the preference for Tuesday is greater than the preference for Monday. Tuesday arrives. Ah, it's preferable to work on this on Wednesday as opposed to Tuesday. Wednesday arrives. Again, it's preferable to work on this Thursday instead of Wednesday. So far, so good; these are transitive relations. Then Thursday arrives. Oops, we think, it is now preferable that we had begun on Monday. This is known as an *intransitive preference*. Chrisoula Andreou, a philosopher at the University of Utah, has argued that when it comes to procrastination, this is a common problem with our thinking.

Certainly, many health behaviors and retirement savings plans suffer from this problem with our reasoning. It comes to a point where tomorrow is not only less preferred, but that an earlier date is actually the preferred date (and it is now too late to act).

Many of us know this relation from experience. Studies from our research group also bear this out. We get a reversal of our preferences that makes for an intransitive preference structure. The problem is that the intransitive nature of this preference structure works against us in the long run. Tomorrow is not as preferable as we once thought.

Our Irrational Thoughts

We often believe things to be true that are not. We do not challenge these beliefs with any reality testing, so they persist. For example, we might believe that we cannot make any mistakes or that we have to be able to answer any and every question after a presentation. We might believe we need to be perfect. We might think that our whole self-worth is dependent upon our career success. All of these are examples of irrational thoughts, and they are common and problematic. They can lead us to experience very negative emotions, and they provide an excuse for not trying. For example, if we are fearful that we cannot do a task perfectly and that our self-worth depends on this perfect performance, then we may avoid the task to protect our self-esteem. We procrastinate.

Manufacturing Our Own Happiness and Resolving Internal Conflict

When our actions and beliefs or even two beliefs are in conflict, they are dissonant. Psychologists call this *cognitive dissonance*. Dissonance is uncomfortable. We want to alleviate this negative state. When we intend to act, when we have a goal toward which we have made an intention to act, and we do not act (voluntarily and quite irrationally choosing to delay action despite knowing this may affect us negatively), we experience dissonance. This dissonance is one of the costs of procrastination.

Here are a few typical reactions that researchers have catalogued as responses to dissonance (and ways that we reduce this dissonance):

1. *Distraction*—we divert our attention away from dissonant cognitions and avoid the negative affective state caused by dissonance.

2. *Forgetting*—can be in two forms, passive and active. Passive is often the case with unimportant thoughts, while we may have to actively suppress important cognitions that are causing dissonance.

3. *Trivialization*—involves changing beliefs to reduce the importance of the dissonance- creating thoughts or beliefs.

4. *Self-affirmation*—creates a focus on our core values and other qualities that reasserts our sense of self and integrity despite the dissonance.

5. *Denial of responsibility*—allows us to distance ourselves as a causal agent in the dissonance.

6. *Adding consonant cognitions*—often by seeking out new information that supports our position (e.g., "this isn't procrastination"; "I need more information before I can do anything on this project").

7. *Making downward counterfactuals*—"it could have been worse"—so we don't learn anything, we just feel better in the short term.

8. *Changing behavior*—to better align with our beliefs and values. This means that we would act instead of procrastinating, although changing one's behavior requires effort and is often not the most convenient way to reduce dissonance.

We are quite expert at employing these strategies to keep buoyant day-to-day. We manufacture our own happiness. It is part of our coping mechanisms.

That said, not all coping mechanisms are adaptive. Quite consistently, research has demonstrated that techniques like distraction, forgetting, trivialization, and denial of responsibility are emotion-focused strategies that are not nearly as effective in the long term as planful problem-solving strategies. Yes, we have to take care of our emotions, but this cannot be where the coping stops. If it is, that is just another instance of giving in to feel good, and we will pay in the long run if this is our dominant short-term strategy.

The Myth of the Arousal Procrastinator

We often hear this: "I work better under pressure." This thinking reflects a sensation seeker of sorts, someone who thrives on pressure. The thing is, our research has shown that this is a myth, at least for the majority of people. Sensation seeking is not related to procrastination, and time pressure typically results in more errors.

Although many people use the excuse that they work better under pressure to explain their needless task delay, it clearly falls into the category above as an example of a rationalization for the dissonance we feel when we fail to act when intended.

Perhaps a more accurate way to rephrase this oft-heard expression is that "we only work under pressure." Why? Most probably because of the mistaken belief, presented in Chapter 4, that our motivational state must match the task at hand. When we do not feel motivated to work on a task, we put it off until finally the external time pressure to do the task motivates action (typically so late that a poorer overall performance is the result).

STRATEGIES FOR CHANGE

I have briefly summarized a number of important biases in our thinking that can get us in trouble. On the one hand, we tend to be overly optimistic about the future and minimize the importance of more distant goals. On the other hand, when it finally comes down to doing something, we prefer tomorrow over today and make excuses about not working to make ourselves feel better. Given these psychological processes, change here is not a simple thing, but it is possible.

Knowledge is power. Recognizing that it is human nature to have these biases, and more important, identifying specifically what we tend to do can be the beginning of change. For example, if we typically say something like "Ah, it's not that important" (trivialization of the goal) or "There's lots of time yet, so I'd prefer to do it tomorrow" (planning fallacy and intransitive preferences), we can learn to make these "flags," or signals for change.

By flag or signal, I mean that as soon as we say something like "There's lots of time, I can do this later," it acts as a trigger or stimulus for a new response. Remember the earlier example of this as an implementation intention? IF we say "Ah, it's not that important," THEN we stop and remind ourselves that this is a form of self-deception, a bias in our thinking, and we just get started on the task instead.

This form of implementation intention puts a cue in the situation (even in our thinking) to help us break a habit. The thought becomes the stimulus for a different response. We break our habitual way of responding. We begin to break that pernicious procrastination habit.

The takeaway for this chapter in terms of what you might do now is to use the space below (or a separate sheet of paper or your computer) to list the things that you commonly say or do to justify your procrastination. You may need to compile this list over the next few days or weeks. The key thing is to learn to recognize how you are reasoning and rationalizing the voluntary, unnecessary delays in your life. Each of these statements can become your own flags to signal a new response.

My typical excuses for rationalizing a needless delay are:

-
-
-
-

If these are your typical rationalizations or excuses for needless task delay, what will your new response be?

In the next chapter, you will see that I think the important step is "just get started." So my standard implementation intention is "IF I say something to myself like 'Oh, I'll feel more like doing this tomorrow,' I will catch myself in this self-deception and add "THEN I will just get started on the task" instead.

It works. You'd be surprised. In the next chapter, I explain why.

6

The Power of Getting Started

◆H◆

Just get started.

I DON'T HAVE TO LOOK very far for a story about this topic. My own life supplies many examples daily. When I face a task that I find aversive, a task I simply don't want to do, a task that I find boring or tedious, or even a task for which I have doubts about my competence, it is tempting to walk away. I want to procrastinate. I find myself saying things like this to myself: "I'll feel more like doing this later." This is a flag for me. It is a signal that I have learned to identify that I am just about to procrastinate. At that very moment, I use this signal to just get started. I will immediately start on anything related to the task at hand. Let's explore why this is so important.

Issue

Once we start a task, it is rarely as bad as we think. Our research shows us that getting started changes our perceptions of a task. It can also change our perception of ourselves in important ways.

In a series of studies, my students and I used electronic pagers to gather what is called experience-sampling data. We paged research participants randomly throughout the day over a week or two. Each time we paged them, we asked things like: "What are you doing?" "Is there something else you should be doing?" "How are you feeling?" "What are you thinking?" In addition, depending on the study, we asked the participants to rate what they were doing and what they were supposed to be doing on things like how stressful they perceived the task to be. A rating of 10 indicated extremely stressful, while a zero meant not stressful at all (and all points in between reflected the variability).

This type of data allowed us to take a sort of snapshot through time of what the participants were doing. Importantly, we also got a real-time glimpse of what they were thinking and feeling. Some of our findings were expected. Some surprised us. I have summarized these findings by simplifying the research as a

Monday-to-Friday process and by focusing mainly on the task avoidance.

As expected, on Monday when participants were avoiding some task(s) (e.g., working on an assignment) in preference to other activities (e.g., hanging out with friends), we found that they typically said things like "I'll feel more like doing that tomorrow" or "Not today. I work better under pressure." As you learned in the previous chapter, we rationalize the dissonance between our behaviors (not doing) and our expectations of ourselves ("I should be doing this now"). Of course, later in the week, none of the participants spontaneously said things like "I feel like doing that [avoided task] today" or "I'm glad I waited until tonight, because I work better like this."

Surprisingly, we found a change in the participants' perceptions of their tasks. On Monday, the dreaded, avoided task was perceived as very stressful, difficult, and unpleasant. On Thursday (or the wee hours of Friday morning), once they had actually engaged in the task they had avoided all week, their perceptions changed. The ratings of task stressfulness, difficulty, and unpleasantness decreased significantly.

What did we learn? Once we start a task, it is rarely as bad as we think. In fact, many participants made comments when we paged them during their last-minute efforts that they wished they had started earlier—the task was actually interesting, and they thought they could do a better job with a little more time.

Just get started. That is the moral here. Once we start, our attributions of the task change. Based on other research, we know that our attributions about ourselves change, too. First, once we get started, as summarized above, we perceive the task as much less aversive than we do when we are avoiding it. Second, even if we do not finish the task, we *have* done something, and the next day our attributions about ourselves are not nearly as negative. We feel more in control and more optimistic. You might even say we have a little momentum.

Research by Ken Sheldon (University of Missouri, Columbia) also demonstrates that progress on our goals makes an important difference. Progress on our goals makes us feel happier and more satisfied with life. Interestingly, positive emotions have the potential to motivate goal-directed behaviors and volitional processes (e.g., self-regulation to stay on task) that are necessary for further goal progress or attainment. Very clearly we can see how if we

"prime the pump" by making some progress on our goals, the re-
sulting increase in our subjective well-being enhances further action and progress.

Of course, this simple advice is not the whole solution to the
procrastination puzzle, but it is a crucial first step toward solving
it and decreasing our procrastination. In the next chapter, I take us
past this initial step.

STRATEGY FOR CHANGE

When you find yourself thinking things like:

"I'll feel more like doing this tomorrow,"
"I work better under pressure,"
"There's lots of time left,"
"I can do this in a few hours tonight" . . .

let that be a flag or signal or stimulus to indicate that you are about
to needlessly delay the task, and let it also be the stimulus to just
get started. This is another instance of that "if . . . then" type of
implementation intention.

I've raised the notion of an implementation intention a few
times already, but I have not provided details about what it is. As
defined in the well-developed psychology of action created by Peter
Gollwitzer (University of New York), an implementation intention

supports a goal intention by setting out in advance when, where, and how we will achieve this goal (or at least a subgoal within the larger goal or task).

It is not as effective to make ourselves a "to do" list of goal intentions as it is to decide how, when, and where we are going to accomplish each of the tasks we need to get done. There is an accumulating body of research by Peter Gollwitzer and his colleagues that demonstrates the efficacy of implementation intentions for initiating behaviors, including following through on the intentions to take vitamins, participating in regular physical activity after surgery, and acting on environmentally minded intentions such as purchasing organically grown foods. In short, implementation intentions are a powerful tool to move from a goal intention to an action.

As I have outlined in earlier chapters, these implementation intentions take the form of "if . . . then" statements. The "if" part of the statement sets out some stimulus for action. The "then" portion describes the action itself. The issue here really is one of a *predecision*. We are trying to delegate the control over the initiation of our behavior to a specified situation without requiring conscious decision.

> IF I say to myself things like "I'll feel more like doing this later" or "I don't feel like doing this now," THEN I will just get started on some aspect of the task.

Notice that we are *not* using the famous Nike slogan of "Just do it!" It's about *just getting started*. The "doing it" will take care of itself once we get going. If we think about "just doing it," we risk getting overwhelmed with all there is to do. If we just take a first step, that is much easier.

As a strategy, you may find that you have to just get started many times throughout the day, even on the same task. This is common. Even in meditation, we have to gently bring our attention back to our focal point, whatever that may be (e.g., our breath, a mantra). The thing to remember is that just getting started may happen many times in a day.

All of our procrastination gets stopped short when we just get started. It is not the whole solution by any means, but it is a huge and crucial first step. As is commonly said, "A job begun is a job half done."

It is tempting to run away from this strategy, to criticize it because it is exactly your problem. You are not able to get started.

Not so. You *think* you are not able to get started, probably because you are focused on your feelings (which are negative), and you are thinking about the whole task, about "getting it done" as opposed to "getting started." The trick is to find something that you can get started on.

Keep it really simple. Keep it as concrete as possible, too. Research by Sean McCrea (University of Konstanz) and his colleagues has shown that thinking abstractly about our goals leads us to believe that they are not that urgent or pressing. More concrete thoughts about your goal or task, more concrete plans, lead to more timely action. In other words, more concrete plans will help you to just get started.

An implementation intention helps you get started. It is your predecision so that you do not get caught up in thinking, choosing, deciding. You have already made the decision. Now is the time to act.

Here is a common example from an academic context: When facing a writing task, perhaps a term paper, it is possible to just sit and stare at a blank computer screen. As you do, anxiety builds, and pretty soon you are giving in to feel good. You are away from your desk another day, and guilt is building fast.

So instead of staring at that blank screen, start typing. Start with a title page. Put your name on it. Add the title if you know it, at least something as a working title. Begin your reference page if you are still not ready to write. Begin jotting down ideas about what you would write about if you could write. You do not have to write sentences, but you can if they come. The thing is, you are now actually working on the task. It is rough, but everything begins that way, rough. Carpenters rough-frame houses. Sculptors carve and shape rough surfaces into smooth ones. Farmers disk and harrow rough, plowed fields into fields ready for planting. We are always starting somewhere to work toward the finished product.

The other way to think about this is the old saying that "a

journey of a thousand miles begins with a single step." Take that first step. Just get started. It can make all the difference.

Honestly, if you are not ready to make this first step, to just get started on a day-to-day, moment-to-moment basis, then put this book down now. You are not committed to change yet, and nothing else I have to say will matter in your self-change. Don't get me wrong, I am not trying to discourage you. I am just being honest.

I will tell you more about other strategies, the role of willpower, and even the effects of our personalities on procrastination in upcoming chapters, but you must know that it will always come down to that precipitous moment when you just get started. It will always come down to that movement from not doing to doing. For tasks that we would rather avoid, this is a difficult but wonderful moment.

So we are back to where I began the chapter, with the mantra "Just get started." To this I have added a couple of other phrases that you might want to use as your own personal mantra. These are: "Prime the pump"; "A job begun is a job half done"; and "A journey of a thousand miles begins with a single step."

In the table that follows (or as a thought experiment), pick a task (or goal) that you are procrastinating on and that is really bothering you. Write down as many of the subtasks that you can think of that are required to get this task done. Now you might use the first column to indicate which subtask is your priority or which subtask makes the most sense for you to complete first. This is the place to just get started. However, even with this list of tasks, you may not know how to proceed. This is simply a reality, and it may not be possible to be completely rational in your approach, but you can still get started. Pick a task, any task, and let that suffice. You may even have to flail around a bit, but if you get started, at least you will find your way. Not starting will guarantee that you will remain stuck. You can take this approach for just about any goal or task that you have.

In fact, when you just cannot seem to get started on a task, get started by breaking down the task into subtasks. BUT don't stop there, as tempting as it may be some days. It is true for many of us that after we make a list like this, we feel better and we think we have accomplished something, so we actually stop—another excuse for procrastination. Don't forget: The purpose of that list is to get you started.

Just get started.

GOAL OR TASK:

PRIORITY OR ORDER OF COMPLETION	LIST OF SUBTASKS

7

Why Getting Started Isn't
the Whole Solution

I need to be prepared to deal with distractions,
obstacles, and setbacks.

HANS HAS REALLY BEEN TAKING his "stop procrastinating" goal to heart. Today, rather than put off work on his report as he typically has, he just got started. He was surprised at how good he felt. He even felt optimistic about the results. Then, about forty-five minutes into his work, the phone rang. Bruce, a friend Hans sees daily, was calling with an invitation to play squash. Bruce's expected partner had canceled at the last minute, so Bruce was hoping Hans would fill in even though they had played the day before. Although

Hans intended to work through the afternoon, to make up for time he'd already lost, he felt like things were under control now, so he told Bruce he would meet him at 12:30 at the gym.

Issue

In the scenario above, Hans's goal was his report, and he made the key first step of getting started. In fact, the night before, Hans had made an implementation intention to begin his work right after he finished breakfast, and he did. He made his predecision with: "If breakfast is done, then I will immediately go to my desk and start working on the third section of my report." Note that he had a concrete task for his action with the "third section" of the report, a section that he felt would be an easy place to begin, even though it was not the beginning of the report itself.

He felt very good about finally doing this. At the very least, there is usually a sense of relief when we get to an avoided task. Unfortunately, these good feelings can be a little bit of a trap for us. They can make us feel overly optimistic, and some of our biases in planning and thinking may begin to emerge. In fact, Hans felt his mind begin to wander, and typical thoughts emerged when he was even a little bit stuck in his progress. At one point when he hit a tough spot in the writing, he caught himself thinking, "Ah, that's enough for today. I'll feel more like doing this part tomorrow." In fact, he was somewhat relieved when Bruce called. It seemed a perfect excuse to stop. Certainly, exercise is important in life, too, he thought.

What this means in terms of more successful goal pursuit is that we have to recognize other points at which we typically abandon our goal pursuit. We have to be prepared to address each of these as they arise; otherwise we will fall back into habitual ways of responding. If you tend to procrastinate more often than you like, then your habitual response will be to find some way to avoid the task at hand.

Procrastination is not just a failure to get started. We can face a variety of problems and needlessly delay action at many stages of goal pursuit. Our feelings may still threaten to derail us. Distractions abound, and it is easy to replace one intention with another, even if just for a minute. And in all of this we can find ways to justify this to ourselves.

In the scenario above, the squash invitation can be seen as an unnecessary disruption given how regularly Hans sees his friend, as well as Hans's intention to work today. Perhaps a more common example for those of us working at our computers is becoming distracted and putting off the task at hand by checking email or surfing the Web. I know from my own research that Internet technologies in particular are potent distracters, as "it will only take a minute to check my email," and then hours later you find you are still off task. I discuss this in more detail in Chapter 10.

What this means is that we cannot simply depend on our goal

intentions, no matter how deeply committed we might be, to keep our volitional actions on track. We have to be prepared to deal with changes in our mood related to setbacks and disappointments. We have to be prepared to deal with distractions. We have to be prepared to overcome obstacles.

Given the ongoing challenges to our goal pursuit, we would benefit from implementation intentions related to the potential distractions and obstacles ahead. We can make predecisions to help us here, too.

STRATEGIES FOR CHANGE

There are two main approaches to predecisions regarding potential distractions. The first involves reducing the number of distractions before we begin to work. The second approach takes us back to implementation intentions to help us decide ahead of time what we will do when distractions, obstacles, or setbacks arise. I outline each of these below.

Minimizing Distractions

Different things distract each of us. Some people cannot work with a radio on in the background or in a noisy room. Others, more extroverted personalities, need that background noise. This means that we have to think about what our typical distractions are.

In a world dominated by computer-related tasks and jobs, certainly some of these distractions are other activities on the computer such as games, social-networking tools, Web searches, or even just email. I discuss these potent distractions under Internet procrastination in the final chapter. For now, I would just add them to our list of potential distractions or obstacles.

The key to this strategy of minimizing distractions is to *be proactive*. Before you begin to work, make sure that you have removed these potential distractions. This might include: shutting your door, shutting off the ringer on the phone, shutting off your cell phone (text messaging is a chronic distraction for many people), shutting down social-networking tools (Facebook, Myspace, Twitter, whatever you use), and removing potentially distracting things from your work space (e.g., magazines, newspapers).

If you reread the paragraph above, you will note that "shutting" is a key verb. You are shutting yourself away from distractions to help maintain your attention and focus on your intended task. This is your predecision to help you work.

Of course, you cannot anticipate *every* distraction, obstacle, or setback in your work. For example, Hans did not expect Bruce to call with the invitation to play squash. You will need another strategy to deal with distractions as they arise. That is the purpose of implementation intentions.

Implementation Intentions

Implementation intentions can work to shield our intentions from competing possibilities, as they can take the form of "If . . . then" statements that anticipate distractions. In fact, experimental research by Peter Gollwitzer and his colleagues has shown that participants who formed temptation-inhibiting implementation intentions outperformed the groups who did not. Importantly, this effect was independent of the participants' motivation to achieve the goal and to ignore distractions.

Implementation intentions have effects over and above our motivation to succeed. This is important. Commitment and motivation alone will not always get us through.

It is time to think about your main procrastinated task(s) again.

In the table that follows (or as a thought experiment), list the kinds of distractions and obstacles that have resulted in further procrastination even when you have actually been working on the task. For each of these, note whether you can remove it prior to task engagement, and/or add an implementation intention as your predecision about how you will act when it arises in the future.

DISTRACTION, OBSTACLE, OR SETBACK	REMOVE PROACTIVELY?	IMPLEMENTATION INTENTION
EXAMPLE: Email	Yes, shut it off before I work.	
EXAMPLE: 'Friends' invitations		IF my friends call to invite me out this weekend, THEN I will immediately say, "Thanks but no, I'm committed to finishing my work."
EXAMPLE: Stuck on my work and don't know what to do		IF I get stuck, confused, and worried because I don't know what to do, THEN I will stay put and list what I do know to be sure what it is I don't know. Once I know this, I can seek help if needed. I won't give up.

8

Willpower, Willpower:
If We Only Had the Willpower

-H

Willpower is a limited resource that I need to use strategically.

RACHEL'S EXERCISE GOAL wasn't becoming a reality. Given her very early start each day to get the kids off to school and out to work herself, she put aside time after dinner to get on the treadmill. However, after an exhausting day in her law firm along with the day-to-day challenges of orchestrating school, day-care schedules, and the many household chores she shares with her husband, she couldn't seem to muster the "get up and go" to get up and go. She was frustrated. She just didn't seem to have the willpower to get off the couch. Every night she put it off again, hoping tomorrow would be different.

Issue

Willpower is a limited resource. I think many of us know this from experience. Roy Baumeister (Florida State University), as well as his students and colleagues, have demonstrated this in a series of clever experiments. It is worth reviewing these to make the point.

In the typical experiment, research participants are randomly assigned to one of two groups. Both groups expect that they will participate in two tasks, but there is an important difference between the groups in terms of the self-regulation demanded of them in the first task.

In the first task, the participants in the *experimental* group are required to self-regulate a great deal, whereas the participants in the *control* group are simply asked to do the task. For example, participants in both groups may be asked to watch a funny film, but the participants in the experimental group would be required to self-regulate by suppressing their emotional expression, while the participants assigned to the control group would be given no specific instructions about how to react. In a similar study, participants in both groups arrive hungry, but the experimental group is invited to eat radishes while resisting a tempting plate of cookies, whereas the control group is allowed to eat the cookies or the radishes (you guess which is more popular). In each of these experiments, the participants in the experimental group exercise self-regulation while the participants in the control group do not.

Once this first task is completed, both groups are asked to complete a second task that involves self-regulation. Participants in both groups need to self-regulate their behavior to achieve success, and the key outcome measure is how persistent participants in each group are. For example, typical second tasks include things like complex figure tracing, solving complex anagrams, drinking an unpleasant (but not harmful) "sports drink," and, my favorite, resisting drinking free beer (a driving test is expected to follow). The main idea is that this second task requires self-regulation, and the hypothesis is that the participants in the experimental group will perform more poorly (not persist as long) because they have already exhausted their ability to self-regulate.

The findings of these studies consistently demonstrate that the participants in the experimental group perform at a lower level than the control group. Given the difference in the self-regulatory demands of the first task, the researchers conclude that the participants in the experimental group have exhausted their self-regulatory strength, at least temporarily, and therefore are unable to muster the self-regulation required for the second task.

In a practical real-life example of this, one study showed that after coping with a stressful day at work, people were less likely to exercise and more likely to do something more passive like watching television. This takes us back to where we began, with Rachel. No wonder she cannot muster the "get up and go" to exercise. She has exhausted her willpower.

Strengthening Our Willpower— The Role of Motivation

The self-regulatory impairments I discussed in the research above are eliminated or reduced when participants are highly motivated to self-regulate on the second task. For example, when participants are paid for doing well on the second task or they are convinced that their performance will have social benefits, they perform well despite the apparent self-regulatory exhaustion from the first task.

The key thing about these findings is that they indicate that self-regulatory depletion may be reducing motivation. Given that depleted self-regulatory strength may leave us feeling like we won't succeed, "we're too tired to try," it may be that the reduced expectancy of success undermines our willingness to exert effort. It's not that we are so impaired that we cannot respond. It's that we "don't feel like it."

Sound familiar? "I'll feel more like it tomorrow." This is a common phrase we use to rationalize our procrastination. Perhaps it simply captures our perceptions of self-regulatory strength at the moment. Of course, it is a perception and, I argue, at least partly an illusion. It's about our motivation to muster the self-regulatory effort—unwilling perhaps, not unable.

From this perspective, what we see is that we may fail to self-regulate because we acquiesce. In the case of procrastination, we find resisting the urge to do something else (an alternative intention) impossible to resist, so we give up and give in.

STRATEGIES FOR CHANGE

We all feel depleted throughout the day. We all have moments where we think, "I'm exhausted and I just can't do any more" or "I'll feel more like this tomorrow." This is true; this is how we are feeling at the moment. However, successful goal pursuit often depends on our moving past these momentary feelings of depletion.

Given the role of motivation in self-regulatory failure, it is crucial to acknowledge the role of higher-order thought in this process, particularly the ability to *transcend the feelings at the moment* in order to focus on our overall goals and values. In the absence of cues to signal the need for self-regulation, we may give in to feel good, and stop trying.

It is exactly when we say to ourselves "I'll feel more like it tomorrow" that we have to stop, take a breath, and think about why we intended to do the task today. Why is it important to us? What benefit is there in making the effort now? How will this help us achieve our goal?

From there, if we can muster the volitional strength for one more step, that is, to "just get started," we will find that we had more self-regulatory strength in reserve than we realized. Our perception can fool us at times, and this self-deception can really be our own worst enemy.

Here are some strategies that you might use to muster what feels like the "fumes" left in your own willpower gas tank.

1. The "willpower is like a muscle" metaphor is a good fit, as the capacity for self-regulation can be increased with regular exercise. Even two weeks of self-regulatory exercise has improved research participants' self-regulatory stamina. So take on some small self-regulatory task and stick to it. This can be as simple as deliberately maintaining good posture or using your nondominant hand to eat. The key element is to exercise your self-discipline. You don't need to start big, just be consistent and mindful of your focus. Over time, you will be strengthening your "willpower muscle."

2. Sleep and rest also help to restore the ability to self-regulate. If you seem to be at the end of your rope, unable to cope and unwilling to do the next task, first *ask yourself if you are*

getting enough sleep. Seven or eight hours of sleep is important for most of us to function well.

3. A corollary to sleep and rest is that self-regulation later in the day is less effective. *Be as strategic as possible,* and don't look to exercise feats of willpower later in the day. (Rachel may have to rethink the timing of her workout or use alternative strategies, suggested below, to help her get off the couch when she is already "running on empty.")

4. A boost of positive emotion has been shown to eliminate self-regulatory impairment. *Find things, people, or events that make you feel good to replenish your willpower strength.*

5. *Implementation intentions can be added to this list of willpower boosters. Make an implementation intention as a plan for action.* As you know, this takes a specific form: "In situation X, I will do behavior Y to achieve my goal Z"; or

SOLVING THE PROCRASTINATION PUZZLE

"If this happens, then I'll do this" (anticipating possible obstacles to your goal pursuit). The effect of these intentions is to put the stimulus for action into the environment and make the control of behavior a nonconscious process. A couple of studies have demonstrated that the automatic nature of the effects of implementation intentions counters the effects of self-regulatory depletion. Let's take the example where research participants had to control their emotions during a humorous movie (suppressing their laughter). As you will recall, they are usually less capable of doing a subsequent experimental task that requires self-regulatory strength, such as solving a series of anagrams. However, for participants randomly assigned to an "if . . . then" implementation intention manipulation, who prepared by saying to themselves, "If I solve an anagram, then I will immediately start to work on the next one," this depletion effect was eliminated (they solved as many anagrams as the group who were not depleted beforehand). This is an interesting result with clear implications for how we can strengthen our flagging willpower at the end of a long day. *An implementation intention may well be the thing that gets you to exercise in the evening, even though you usually feel much too tired to begin.* Note: This research underscores my focus on just get started. I think Rachel might be more successful with her evening exercise if she had the implementation intention of "If the kids are in bed, then I will go directly to the treadmill." Once she starts, she might discover that she has the motivation and energy that she needs.

6. Self-regulation appears to depend on available blood glucose. In some studies, even a single act of self-regulation has been shown to reduce the amount of available glucose in the bloodstream, impairing later self-regulatory attempts. Interestingly, just a drink of sugar-sweetened lemonade eliminated this self-regulatory depletion in experiments. Even though this research hasn't always been replicated, the message is clear: *Don't get hypoglycemic; your self-regulation will suffer. Keep a piece of fruit (complex carbohydrate) handy to restore blood glucose.*

7. Be aware that social situations can require more self-regulation and effort than you may think. For example, if you are typically an introverted person but you have to act extroverted, or you have to suppress your desired reaction (scream at your boss) in favor of what is deemed more socially acceptable (acquiesce again to unreasonable demands), you will deplete your willpower for subsequent action. These social interactions may even make it more likely that you will say or do something you will regret in

subsequent interactions. *Getting along with others requires self-regulation, so you will need to think about points 1–6 to be best prepared to deal with demanding social situations.*

8. Finally, *so much of our ability to self-regulate depends on our motivation.* Even on an empty stomach, exhausted from not enough sleep and pushed to the limit for self-regulation, we can muster the willpower to continue to act appropriately. It is difficult, but it can be done, particularly if we focus on our values and goals to keep perspective on more than just the present moment. In doing this, we can transcend the immediate (and temporary) feelings we are having to keep from giving in to feel good, which lies at the heart of so much self-regulatory failure.

9

What's Bred in the Bone: Personality and Procrastination

✦

My personality might put me at risk, but I can adapt.

FIONA AND DAVID have been married for more than ten years now. Fiona's friends describe her as organized. Typically, she's the planner in their group, and they know that they can really count on her. When there's something to be done, she does it right away. David sets high standards for himself. He is also very self-critical. He seems to hear his parents' voices echo in his mind whenever he approaches a task, saying, "It could be better." When faced with a task, David always seems reluctant to get started. Fiona and David are very similar when it comes to household tidiness (they are both quite particular, even fussy), but they can drive each other crazy at times when it comes to scheduling and doing tasks.

Issue

The example above highlights the notion of individual differences. We might think of Fiona as conscientious and David as a perfectionist. This approach to personality is based on the concept of personality traits.

Traits are terms that psychologists use to summarize the way we typically act. Traits describe something about how we expect a person to act in most situations. Of course, how we actually behave depends on both personality and situation, but for the moment, I want to focus on personality traits.

Certainly, procrastination has been shown to be related to personality traits. Some people are more prone to procrastinate, and a contributing factor is personality. This is particularly true when the situational pressures to engage in a task in a timely manner are not strong. When the situation is not pushing us to act in a certain way (for example, a supervisor actually monitoring our actions), our personality will have a great deal of influence on our behavior.

The examples above provide two very common traits related to procrastination, but in different directions. Fiona's conscientiousness—that is, the fact that she is typically organized, planful, and dutiful—is a trait that is highly *negatively* related to procrastination. The more we are conscientious, the less we typically procrastinate.

In contrast, David is an example of a socially prescribed perfectionist. Yes, there are different varieties or types of perfectionism. The one we need to focus on is the socially prescribed perfectionist, because it is most strongly related to procrastination. Socially prescribed perfectionists believe that others hold unrealistic expectations for their behavior and that they cannot live up to these expectations. They experience external pressure to be perfect and believe that others evaluate them critically. This leads them to internalize these expectations and be self-critical as well (that "little voice in David's head" is an example of this internalized criticism).

Contrasting Fiona and David like this shows how personality can be a resilience or risk factor for procrastination. We need to take this into account in our own lives.

Would you say that you have a procrastination-prone personality?

To answer this question, you need to have a little more information about which personality traits have been shown to be associated with procrastination. Some of the key traits that are related to procrastination are listed below. I just need to make one more comment before you review this list.

There are potentially thousands of personality traits. Personality psychologists have simplified these into a superstructure of traits known as the "Big Five." Much like the three colors of the color wheel, the Big Five are said to be the primary traits. Other traits are a part of these five or a blend of them. You can remember the five traits with the mnemonic CANOE: Conscientiousness, Agreeableness, Neuroticism, Openness (to Experience), and Extraversion.

Of course, in a digest-type book, I cannot explain each of these in detail, and it is really not that important because our focus is on procrastination. Research pioneered by Henri Schouwenburg (University of Groningen) and Clarry Lay (York University) has revealed that only two of these traits have meaningful relations with procrastination—Conscientiousness and Neuroticism (which is also known as Emotional Instability). I discuss these first below.

The other traits that I discuss below are related to the Big Five traits, but I address them separately because they deserve special consideration given their relation to procrastination. For example, impulsiveness is sometimes discussed as part of low emotional stability, sometimes extraversion. In any case, it is not necessary to focus on these definitional issues. Just think of these traits as aspects of our personalities.

INSTRUCTIONS

For each of the traits below, rate yourself from "Not at all like me"
to "Exactly like me" on how much you think the trait describes you.

1. Conscientiousness

Highly conscientious people are described as responsible, scrupulous, persevering, and fussy or tidy. You can see how this trait is negatively associated with procrastination and might be considered a resilience factor against unnecessary delay. The various facets of the trait as measured in popular personality tests include: Competence (efficient), Order (organized), Dutifulness (not careless), Achievement striving (thorough), Self-discipline (not lazy), and Deliberation (not impulsive).

I am a very conscientious person.

1	2	3	4	5	6	7	8	9	10
Not at all like me									*Exactly like me*

2. Emotional instability

Emotional instability is the alternative wording of the trait of Neuroticism. People who score high on emotional instability can be described as nervous, worrisome, or anxious. The various facets of the trait as measured in popular personality tests include: Anxiety (tense), Angry hostility (irritable), Depression (not contented), Self-consciousness (shy), Impulsive (moody), and Vulnerability (not self-confident).

Typically, I would consider that I am more neurotic or less emotionally stable than others.

1	2	3	4	5	6	7	8	9	10

Not at all like me   *Exactly like me*

3. Impulsiveness

A person who scores high on impulsiveness tends to act before thinking. This trait reflects low self-control, especially in the presence of potentially rewarding activities. Impulsivity reflects less ability to consider the consequences of one's actions.

Typically, I would say that I am very impulsive.

1	2	3	4	5	6	7	8	9	10

Not at all like me   *Exactly like me*

4. Self-efficacy

This trait represents the belief that we are able to do what is necessary to achieve a desired outcome. It reflects self-confidence and competence.

I feel that I am competent and have a great deal of self-efficacy.

1	2	3	4	5	6	7	8	9	10

Not at all like me   *Exactly like me*

(continued)

5. Self-esteem

Self-esteem is how we feel about ourselves. It is our appraisal of our self-worth. Another way to think about it is the extent to which we perceive ourselves as being relatively close to being the people we want to be.

Generally, I feel very good about myself.

1	2	3	4	5	6	7	8	9	10

Not at all like me   *Exactly like me*

6. Socially prescribed perfectionism

As I noted, socially prescribed perfectionists believe that others hold unrealistic expectations for their behavior. They believe that others expect them to be perfect, and they can feel compelled to try to live up to these expectations.

I believe that significant others in my life expect me to be perfect.

1	2	3	4	5	6	7	8	9	10

Not at all like me   *Exactly like me*

Now that you have reviewed some of the main personality traits that researchers have identified as traits associated with procrastination, you can see which is larger, your risk for or resilience to procrastination. To calculate each, you need to sum items together as listed below. For each item, write in the number you circled when reading above, then sum these for a total score out of a possible 30.

Personality Risk: → Sum items #2 _____ + #3 _____ + #6 _____ = _____

(Emotional Instability, Impulsiveness, Perfectionism)

Personality Resilience: → Sum items #1 _____ + #4 _____ + #5 _____ = _____

(Conscientiousness, Self-Efficacy, Self-Esteem)

This simple scale is not scientifically valid, but it does provide you with a rough estimate of your vulnerability to procrastination from a personality perspective. These scores provide an index in terms of how your personality is contributing to or protecting you from self-regulation failure. Of course, given that you are reading a book about procrastination, I might assume that you are more at risk than resilient. You may find that your risk score is quite a bit larger than your resilience score. The question is, what can you do about this?

STRATEGY FOR CHANGE

Personality presents an interesting challenge when we think about self-change. By definition, we consider personality as the relatively enduring characteristics of the individual. They are not easily changed.

However, we do not have to change our personalities to succeed. We can act counter to our dispositions or traits. For example, there are many introverted individuals who can function well socially, speak in front of crowds, and engage others effectively in the workplace. It does take strategic effort at times, but we are successful daily "acting out of character."

It is important to acknowledge that some psychologists believe that acting out of character, counter to our traits and disposition, can deplete our self-regulatory strength or willpower. As we discussed previously, willpower is a limited resource, so this is important to recognize. We will be investing our energies to act out of character to succeed. Everything noted earlier about bolstering our willpower will be important to take into account as you work to address your personality risk factors.

In terms of procrastination, it is possible to act out of character in terms of low conscientiousness or high impulsivity. The key thing is to be strategic, and as we have discussed, part of being strategic is making predecisions about how to respond before you face a situation. If you can be proactive like this, you will not rely so much on your personality and habitual ways of responding.

Remember the implementation intentions discussed earlier? These are intentions that take the form of "In situation X, I will do behavior Y." Implementation intentions, as you may recall, are a form of predecision. You are deciding ahead of time what will be a stimulus for what response.

You may find implementation intentions useful again in terms of counteracting a habitual response that is part of who you are as defined by these personality traits. For example, if you are rather impulsive, your predecision with an implementation intention might be "If an alternative intention arises, such as an invitation to go out, I will say that I will make my decision in ten minutes." This built-in predecisional delay may help to counteract the typical impulsive response to just get going.

I think it is clear by now that the key issue is this predecision. Knowing a little bit about your personality traits that may put you at risk to procrastinate, you can now act on that knowledge by deciding in advance how you will counter this habitual response.

For example, if you are impulsive, it is particularly important to reduce distractions in the surrounding environment when you are trying to work. Impulsive people have more difficulty resisting these distractions, even with implementation intentions. So, as I discussed in a previous chapter, part of your predecisional process can be to eliminate or reduce the distractions before you get down to work.

Similarly, if you tend to be disorganized, deliberately working on structuring tasks can be very important to reducing procrastination. This can be as simple as creating a "to do" list of subtasks that help you see the steps you need to take. It can also be the more challenging job of organizing your work area so that it is not so cluttered. But be careful: Some of us use this tidy-up job as our way to procrastinate! Once the desk is tidied, pencils sharpened, and new software downloaded onto the computer, we think, "That's enough for today!" Procrastination draws on our ability to deceive ourselves. We find excuses for just about any unnecessary delay.

The strategies above address the issues of impulsivity and conscientiousness. What about the worry and anxiety that define low emotional stability? What if we are worried that we don't have the ability to do the task? What if we cannot tolerate frustration? This seems more serious, right?

Yes, some of us are prone to worry and self-consciousness, and many of us have irrational beliefs that make us prone to procrastinate. Our procrastination may be based on a fear of failure, for example. The route to self-change, both in the short term behaviorally and the long term in terms of stable personality change, is to challenge your worries and beliefs as they arise. When a task triggers thoughts such as "I can't do this," "I'm such a screwup," "I don't know how," "I'm going to fail," it's absolutely essential that you challenge each of these beliefs. Why do you think they are true? What is the real risk of not succeeding when you try? Through this process, most of us realize that these are truly irrational thoughts, perhaps part of the habits we call personality, but not real in terms of the world around us.

In sum, I am arguing that these stable individual differences we call personality traits can contribute to our procrastination. We cannot make changes in these traits quickly or easily, but we can recognize our relative self-regulatory strengths and limitations. In doing this, we set ourselves up to act more proactively and consciously out of character as we may need to achieve our goals.

Perhaps most important to understand is that personality should not be an excuse. In fact, acknowledging and addressing our limitations can develop some of our greatest strengths.

10

Cyberslacking on the
Procrastination Superhighway

*"It will only take a minute" puts me on a slippery
slope toward procrastination.*

IT'S APPROACHING MIDNIGHT and Ari still hasn't started to work on his report, even though he sat down at his computer at 7 p.m. When he got to his desk earlier that evening, his intention had been to get to work, but he thought, "I'll just update my Facebook status—it will only take a minute." Now, hours later, he's still there.

Issue

I have included this short chapter because Internet-based technologies and other forms of technologically mediated communication, like smartphones, have created a whole new world of time wasting. There is little doubt that our best tools for productivity—computer technologies—are potentially also one of our greatest time wasters. In fact, the title of this chapter was taken from one of the published papers from our research group. In this paper, published more than a decade ago (long before social-networking tools became popular), our participants reported that 47 percent of their time online was spent procrastinating. I think this is a conservative estimate.

I doubt that I have to write very much to convince you that the Internet has the potential to waste time if you want it to. People I know bemoan this fact all the time. The best example I have in relation to this chapter is a reply to one of my *Psychology Today* blog posts. In response to the "it will only take a minute" theme, an anonymous reader wrote:

> im procrastinating . . . that's why im here . . . i just google things im
> thinking about, like this . . . or like i hear someone hum a familiar tune, so
> i look up the song to know who sang it . . . i mean that LITERALLY takes a
> minute, but then that makes me google a couple other things and then it
> ends up lasting a lot more than a few minutes . . . and i honestly dont

realize when i end up reading the wikipedia page of some random disease that some singer had that was related to the singer i was looking up. wait, why was i looking him up? oh right, cos someone at my school was humming a song by him. . . . . oh right, school. . . . . essay due tomorrow, haven't started.

   like right now, i just realized . . . im commenting on an article. . . . . i wish i could read those articles about my essay and try to get 2000 words on paper in a day.

The thing is, we can end up wasting time even when we do not want to. This is the real problem, and one that we need to identify in order to make change.

I just want to be clear about something. I am not saying we cannot work and play online. Personally, I really enjoy these technologies—I use them intensively, in fact—and I know we will see them grow in importance. What I am emphasizing is that we can waste time in unexpected and unanticipated ways with these technologies *when we don't want to.* This is the issue. These technologies are particularly problematic when it comes to self-regulation and self-regulation failure.

In the scenario above, Ari did plan to work on his report. He got to his desk as planned. What happened?

Ari made a rational decision over an irrationally short period of time. Although it is correct that it might take only a minute to "update my Facebook page," a minute later Ari faced the same decision. Of course, as we learned in Chapter 5, our thinking can let us down here. We can rationalize yet another minute of delay, as another minute will certainly not compromise the report writing. It is an intransitive preference at its best, isn't it? At midnight, Ari recognizes that it is preferable to act much sooner than he has (even though each minute prior to that, he preferred to delay just a little more).

This issue of rational decisions over irrationally short periods of time, combined with problems in our thinking like intransitive preferences, is not the only reason that the Internet and social networking in particular are potentially so hazardous to our goal pursuit. There are other reasons that we are prone to procrastinate online.

1. One of the reasons that social networking is so rewarding is that it fulfills a basic human need, at least at some level. That is the need for relatedness. We are social animals, and social networking makes sense.

2. Online social networking is also immediately rewarding. This is a potentially addictive combination—*rewarding and immediate*. In fact, there is a great deal written about Internet addictions. Although it is beyond the scope of my writing to delve into this topic, it is important to note that the powerfully addictive nature of the Internet contributes

to the self-regulation failure that you now understand is at the heart of procrastination. It can undermine our best intentions.

3. A third reason that the Internet can be a problem for procrastination is that it is a ready distraction, which is particularly troublesome for those of us who are impulsive. In fact, it can be a problem for all of us because of so many "push technologies." For example, email and text messages are pushed to us throughout the day, so as we work, we can be constantly interrupted if we leave our email client and phone active in the background. These distractions can be exceptionally disruptive at moments when our on-task work is not going well. Then we are back to that "it will only take a minute to . . ." and our goal pursuit ends in favor of tasks that we really are not choosing to do, at least not in the long run (although it can end up that way, to our detriment).

4. On top of all of this is the myth of multitasking. I say myth because despite popular beliefs, research indicates that only a very small percentage of people can actually multitask effectively. Humans have a very limited attentional channel. We are better off focused on one thing at a time. Tragic traffic accidents are only one example of how potentially dangerous the myth of

multitasking can be as texting drivers lose their focus on the road. The more mundane tragedy of multitasking is how we deceive ourselves into thinking that we are actually doing our work when in fact we are attending sporadically to our tasks in between email, social-networking updates, Internet searches, ecommerce, and gaming.

STRATEGIES FOR CHANGE

Although I discuss the procrastination superhighway as a separate chapter in this book, the principles for change are not really that different. They may just be a whole lot less appealing. For example, we have already addressed the notion of minimizing distractions when we discussed impulsivity. Minimizing distractions is part of that predecision to keep us on task.

Minimizing distractions is an important part of curbing our online procrastination. To stay really connected to our goal pursuit, we need to disconnect from potential distractions like social-networking tools. This means that we should not have Facebook, Twitter, email, or whatever your favorite suite of tools is running in the background on your computer or smartphone while you are working. Shut them off.

Ouch. I know—it is really tempting to find some excuse to keep it a "business as usual" approach here, but if you are committed to reducing your procrastination, this is something you really need to do. You must shut off everything except the program you need on your computer to do the task at hand. This means you can plan your "ebreaks" more consciously—again, this is an example of predecisions that help us break unconscious habits. Procrastination is certainly a habit for many of us.

This strategy of reducing distractions makes it more obvious when you are turning away from your goal pursuit to pursue some other task. Your alternative and potentially rewarding alternative tasks are no longer only a click away. A little more effort provides time for you to think if this is really what you want to do. Do you really want to abandon your goal right now? Probably not.

There have been all sorts of tools and "apps" designed to help people regulate their Internet use more. Common current examples include tools that lock you out of your email or record what applications you are using and for how long. These may be helpful to you, but techniques and technologies can never be a substitute for a commitment to change.

I think it is appropriate to end this final chapter where I began our consideration of why we procrastinate—giving in to feel good. Giving in to feel good is a big piece of the procrastination puzzle, and the Internet provides lots and lots of short-term, but specious, rewards to which we can give in to feel good.

With a click or two we can leave the task that we feel bad about

SOLVING THE PROCRASTINATION PUZZLE

and seek immediate mood repair. If you understand that this is what you are doing, you are truly on the road to change.

That does not mean that this is easy, and I turn now to some thoughts about the road ahead. It is a journey that is often described as "two steps forward, one step back."

Concluding Thoughts:
On the Road of Self-Change

✦

Self-change is a journey I take daily, and I will persevere patiently as I take two steps forward and one step back.

MARIANNA IS DISCOURAGED. Yesterday went so well. She started her work exactly when she intended to and she stayed on task. It felt great. She made significant progress on her thesis. Today she feels like her old self. She doesn't want to do anything. She's already wasted the morning filing email (most of which she knows she'll never look at again) and texting friends. Feeling low on energy, she's thinking of having a nap after lunch. Deep down she knows she's just avoiding her work again.

Issue

Even though the purpose of the digest format of this book is to make it a quick read, there are no quick fixes. Our old bad habits, like procrastination, are hard to change and new habits are difficult to establish. We have to put in a great deal of conscious effort before our new behaviors become routine, nonconscious patterns in our lives. Sometimes we never completely establish a new habit, and we have to put in conscious effort daily to maintain our focus where we choose.

The key thing is to be strategic. By being strategic, by making predecisions as much as possible, we can keep from following the same old worn path, the path that we know best as procrastination.

As you have learned, there are many aspects of being human that contribute to our self-regulation failure. For example, we:

- like to feel good now,
- are prone to discount future rewards,
- are overly optimistic and biased in our planning,
- dislike dissonance and will resolve it by making excuses,
- have a limited amount of willpower,
- can be disorganized, undisciplined, and overly self-conscious,

- can be prone to distractions, and
- can have irrational beliefs about our expectations of ourselves.

Each of these things can create problems for us in our goal pursuit and contribute to our procrastination. And even this partial list of factors contributing to procrastination reveals some important truths worth remembering when you feel like Marianna does in the scenario above.

First, each of us will have a different constellation of factors that is our recipe for procrastination. As you read this book, I am sure that some topics and issues spoke more directly to you than others. These are the issues that you need to address in your efforts for self-change. These are the issues you can address beginning right now.

Second, we cannot change everything at once. My emphasis has been on being strategic. You need to be strategic in your approach to self-change as well. Pick one or two issues that you recognize are problems for you. Review the chapter on these issues, if necessary, and focus on those strategies first. You can build from there.

Third, this self-change process is uneven. We truly do feel like one day we leap ahead and the next day we fall back. Although we have to be committed to change and firm in our efforts to be strategic, we also have to be kind to ourselves during this challenging process. We all face setbacks, disappointing moments, and frustrations with our apparent lack of progress. Your attitude toward these setbacks and yourself will be extremely important to your continued progress. Be kind but firm with yourself, and be willing to forgive yourself when you do not live up to your own expectations.

One of our recent studies was about this issue of self-forgiveness and procrastination. It has important implications for each of us as we take the self-change journey. What we found was that self-forgiveness for procrastination was related to less procrastination in the future. Specifically, when students in our study had procrastinated quite a bit on their preparation for an exam, if they self-forgave for this procrastination, they were less likely to procrastinate on their preparation for the subsequent exam.

This finding reflects the power of forgiveness to move us from an avoidance motivation to an approach motivation. If, for example, you had a transgression (e.g., fight or broken promise) with a friend, and you or your friend had not offered forgiveness, you would likely avoid that friend. In the case of procrastination, the transgression is against the self, and we end up avoiding the task associated with that transgression. What forgiveness does in both cases is to remove the avoidance motivation so that friendship can be reestablished or engagement with the task can happen again, respectively.

On our self-change journey, we have to be prepared to forgive ourselves for our transgressions so that we are willing to try again.

We will certainly have to try again many times. As I said before, even my simple strategy of just get started may have to be invoked many times throughout the day. Start and restart.

Success will be found in this effort. It is worth the effort, as was your time in considering why it is we that procrastinate. I hope reading this book is your first step in this journey of self-change.

I would love to hear about your own journey. What worked? What didn't? What else would you like to know? Although I cannot promise to answer every email, your input will make a difference to future writing. I invite you to write to me at tpychyl@procrastination.ca.

Finally, you may want to learn more about procrastination. This digest-format book, while accurate and firmly based on research in the area, is by necessity short on details. If you want to learn more, you can find lots more through our research group Web site: procrastination.ca.

This Web site provides access to many relevant resources, not just our own scholarly publications. Perhaps some of the most accessible information is available through my "Don't Delay" blog for *Psychology Today* and through my iProcrastinate Podcasts. The blog entries and podcast episodes summarize a wide variety of information about procrastination in much greater detail. In fact, you can search through the blog entries or the podcast titles on iTunes to find information specific to the issues with which you may be struggling.

I must say that I make this reference to further reading with some reservation. There is no end to reading about a topic, and the problem with procrastination, as you have learned, is that we can always find an excuse not to do our work. In this case, it is really quite possible to use your further reading and research about procrastination to procrastinate more! Ironically, this is something that readers of my blog and listeners of my podcasts have told me that they do.

So, instead of reading more, I would have you return to where I began the book to remind you that reducing procrastination in our lives is a practical thing—sensible, realistic, no-nonsense. In addition, I want to add that change is about doing, not just reading. If you put these both together, you will see that the practical (and no-nonsense) thing is to start doing, not to read more.

You probably took an interest in this book because you want to reduce procrastination in your life. You now know a great deal more about the topic. You are prepared to bolster what feels like a depleted willpower. You are aware that it is tempting to give in to feel good, so you won't right now. And you know that every journey begins with that important first step.

It is time to *just get started*. I know that this will make a difference in your life.